Going Vertical:

Acrostics
in Action

Linda Ann Nickerson

Gait
House
Press

Published in the United States by Gait House Press.

Printed in the United States of America.

2021

Cover and internal illustration/s: *Country Girl Leaning Against a Ladder,* by Silvestro Lega (c1885). Public domain image.

ISBN: 978-1-7371383-2-7

GOING VERTICAL: ACROSTICS IN ACTION

Going Vertical:

Acrostics in Action

GOING VERTICAL: ACROSTICS IN ACTION

Dedication

Going Vertical: Acrostics in Action is dedicated to a lengthy list of long-suffering friends who have cheerfully endured my whirlwinds of wordplay over the years.

You've heard me fiddle with phrasings, deal in double entendres, put on puns, dabble in descriptions, wrestle with rhymes, and angle for alliterations.

Your appreciation, interest, and appreciation (real or feigned, and typically in that order) have propelled me to produce poetry at all.

Many thanks.

GOING VERTICAL: ACROSTICS IN ACTION

Table of Contents

Introduction

What does it mean to go vertical?

This simple phrase may be anything but simple. Going vertical, on the surface, probably points to upward progress in some form.

If we're moving ahead, then we must be going vertical.

On the other hand, anyone who is still vertical presently possesses what it takes to proceed. If you're holding this book, then you're clearly vertical (at least, in some form).

Like the subject of the cover artwork, we may find ourselves leaning against life's proverbial ladder from time to time, rather than climbing it. But we're still going vertical.

And it sure beats horizontal.

Going vertical takes tons of turns.

This gathering of acrostic verses represents a miscellany of myriad moods, memories, and mindsets.

Some of these poems may seem

straightforward or somewhat silly, while others are symbolic or spiritual. A smattering are sort of sarcastic. Inclusions range from merry to melancholy, angry to amused, and wispy to weighty.

Although not all the verses in this volume are expressly upbeat in nature, the hope is that any form of inspiration, edification, or authenticity draws both reader and writer upwards in some way.

Poetry can be playful or purposeful. Most often, it's a bit of both.

Acrostics have been called alphabetic poetry.

Mainly, that's because this poetic form focuses on key words' initials for its format.

On the other hand. one might say this particular anthology of acrostic poems runs the gamut, all the way from A to Z. It actually does! The list includes acrostic poems representing every letter of the alphabet.

That's primarily why this acrostic anthology is arranged alphabetically.

Also, this book contains a fair number of acrostic poems that have appeared earlier in various publications (from magazines to textbooks) or on my own poetry blog. However, the lion's share of these verses are seen here for the first time.

Acrostic poetry formats vary.

Although the basic poetic principle (using line-opening letters to form key word topics/titles of acrostic poems) carries throughout, these verses vary in many structural ways.

Some are short, while others fill full pages. Several are simple, free-form poems, but plenty more of these verses contain specific structures (such as rhyme and meter).

Readers will even find five-line limericks employing the acrostic form.

Must a poet's poems all blend with one another?

One of the intriguing features of a poem is that it may be open to multiple interpretations.

Gather plentiful poems by a single writer in a collection (as here), and the reader may even sense a jumble of contradictions scattered about. Perhaps that is the perception of the reader. But it also may be that each poem merely captures the writer in a single snapshot of his or her life journey.

The poet's life is in process, like any other's.

Scores of writers work through their own questions with their words. We may try wide-ranging ideas on for size before moving on. We form our faith, balance our beliefs, slug out our stresses, and walk out our worries in verse.

Sometimes we simply blow off steam.

Hence, what appears to be a mixed message may not be so at all.

Poetry comes from plentiful places.

It's dangerous to assume a poet only writes autobiographically.

Verses may arise from the writer's own experience. They can also come from stories shared in passing or penetrating conversations. Or they may be wholly fiction or fantasy, arising from the poet's imagination.

No poetic finger-pointing is intended.

If a reader should find him or herself somehow in any of the lines that follow, it's simply serendipity.

Or it may be because some observations are widely (or even universally) transferrable.

No actual personal identifications are aimed (for credit or cost), so please read on with glasses of grace.

We're all going vertical; let's keep it on the up-and-up.

So here's to you, from A to Z.

GOING VERTICAL: ACROSTICS IN ACTION

Advice Corner

Absolute abounds;
Don't have to ask –
Vicariously up to task.
I dare not share,
'Cause everywhere
Each ear unfolds to make a mask.

Can anyone concede, admit
Our own occurrences permit –
Returning unsought wisdom cheap
Negates relating ever-deep?
Engaging though our thoughts be geared,
Remarks may pale when volunteered.

Angels and Demons

Absolute opposites
Never negate
Genetic ties.
Eternity calls.
Look and learn.
See the similarities.

Animosities endure,
Never knowing
Dominion is done.

Dare they defy
Everlasting order.
Mounting their mettle
Over the heavenlies?
Now and forever,
Sovereignty is unchanged.

Ants in Your Pants

Arrhythmic staccato,
Numbly prancing,
Timeless dancing.
Sinews spring to action.

Interruptions
Never know order.

Yelling and yammering.
Outbursts unceasing.
Undercurrents of impatience,
Rumbling repeatedly.

Put that down.
Afterwards, not now.
No. No. No.
Time to sit still.
Stop it. Can't.

As Good As It Gets

Anyone can
See.

Greatest gifts
Outdo all
Others.
Don't they?

Anyone can
See.

Identity travels not
Two-by-two.

Go grab life.
Enjoy enthusiastically.
Today awaits each
Single soul.

Autumn

As the days begin to fade
Underneath a cloudy shade,
Tumbling leaves will start to twirl.
Using rakes, each boy and girl
Makes a mound to jump and play.
Naked winter's on the way.

Back Seat Driver

Belted-in bellower,
Always alarmed,
Cries for control.
Kids are comical.

Stop right there.
Eateries everywhere.
Attention-getting alerts
Tempt tiny taste buds.

"Don't drive by.
Remember you promised
I'd have a snack?"
Values are vital,
Even for parents.
Ruling from the child seat?

Back to Square One

Biding time
After achievement,
Can crusaders
Kill creativity?

Try triumph
On for size.

Suddenly conquests
Quit.
Unseen underlings
Acquiesce.
Ready or not, all is
Erased.

Only, if only,
Necessity had knocked.
Everything begins again.

Bandwidth

Basically,
Assumptions
Need to
Drop
When
Idea-overload
Diminishes
Topped-out
Headspace.

Banquet

Bounteous banquet,
Awash in color,
Needs no menu.
Quintessential quest
Unmeasured,
Every appetite is
Tested by treats.

Banshee

Biting banshees
Always attack
Needlessly.
Shark-like, they
Hover to
Eat the innocent with
Evil enjoyment.

Beacon

Beckon, beacon.
Enlighten us.
Along the rocky shore, with
Crashing waves along the coast,
Only your shine can signal us to safety.
Now we need you more than ever.

Beast of Eden

Belly scraping garden bed,
Eden's bully built his dread.
Angling for spot to snap,
Serpent stirred her from her nap.
"Taste and see," he pretty pled.

"Off you go," she did dispute.
"Flee with your forbidden fruit."

End of tale, the lass partook.
Dined with Adam, reads the book.
Evil came to challenge glory,
Now there's much more to the story.

Best Boy

Beauty and
Elegance,
Safe and sound –
Trotting with try.

Bay boy,
Outstanding in his field,
Yet or evermore.

Benign

Bulging blob,
Egging on edginess,
Never to nod.
Ignominious.
Going, gone.
Neutralized.

Blind

Blind, I've been.
Lost one eye's sight.
It left, returned,
Neurons in flight.
Dear nerves, hold tight.

Brainstorm

Beyond all notions we have known,
Remarkable ideas are shown.
An atmospheric freedom waits,
Inspiring ever widening gates.
No boundaries may block our way;
Still forth we step, as step we may.
Tomorrow's truths may telegraph.
Our colleagues twitter, taunt and laugh.
Reject the ridicule, and stand.
Mere brainstorms grow to concepts grand.

Breaking Up

Bypassing
Respect,
Esteem is
Absolutely
Knotted
Into
Ninety little lies –
Gone.

Unstung?
Perhaps.

Breathe

Bask.
Relax.
Enjoy.
Allow.
Taste
Heaven,
Even now.

Broken Verses

Busted.
Ruined.
Objects of nil.
Killing time and
Erasing lines of
Needless nouns.

Vibrant verses
Escape,
Replaced by
Silly sentences and
Empty phrasings.
Stop awhile, Muse.

Burger

Browse the menu;
Unfold each page.
Read each option;
Guess and gauge.
Examine options in every size;
Return to order a burger and fries.

Call It Even

Conflict
Always
Leaves
Losers.

It's
Time.

Each is a
Victim,
Except those who
Negotiate.

Call of the Mild

Could be the least
Are found to feast
Long past the hour
Life goes sour.

Observe. Attend.
Find favor, friend.

The ones who barge
Head-first and large
Emerge in charge.

Maybe that's so.
It seems. I know.
Look up and view
Deliv'rance due.

Candidates

Conflict and chaos send voters awhirl,

As contrary claims are debunked, truth grows
muddled.

No ballots yet counted, but we've come hinged.

Don't we know better by now?

It's clear the world's gone topsy-turvy.

Debaters dig deep for dirt, and vice-versa.

Ask anybody. Even the future's door is turned
upside down.

Time for a reset. We're not gonna find a Savior
on the ballot.

Everything changes when we realize this isn't
really our home.

Suppose we remember the Lord isn't running
for President.

Catnap

Curled and contorted on the couch,
Along beside me snores a grouch.
Time slips away, but stir she won't.
No, don't disturb her. Dare you don't.
Awake, she'll hiss and bare her teeth.
Perhaps she's puma underneath.

Celebration

Convening cheerfully,
Everyone is exuberant.
Look all around.
Entertainment and excellent eats
Beckon us to indulge.
Relationships are reborn,
And acquaintances are established.
Time travels too quickly.
Instants escape us.
Overdue outlooks elapse.
No wonder we lose touch.

Chasing Rainbows

Calling from a field of blue,
Heaven's ribbons
Alight above.
Shining fairly
In a fragile light,
Naming a promise of storm's end.
Glimpses of glory are revealed.

Reigning unquestioned,
Almighty paints His wonders
In the firmament.
Now we know
Benevolence exists
Over all.
What beauty
Still remains.

Coffee Break

Cup of Joe
On the run.
Frothy,
Foamy –
Everyone's
Enjoying.

Back to work;
Race, return.
Exit,
Anguish,
Know the burn.

Confess

Coming clean's
Only option
Needs to know
Forgiveness.
Every exception
Stops short, till
Someone saves us.

Crime Scene

C'mon now.
Recognize rights.
I'm not an alibi.
Make your merry,
Exercising exemptions.

Someone sees.
Can you comprehend?
Even here,
Number's up.
Entitlement is ending.

Drama

Desperately destroying
Roles that run well.
All about anger
Made more by mere mention.
Alert, she aims her arrows.

Earphones

Enter
At your own
Risk,
People.
Here I sit,
Only focused,
Needing to concentrate,
Earphones in place –
Still haven't connected the cord.

Extra

Every
eXcuse
Trained to
Regain
Attention.

Extra! Extra!

Extra! Extra! Read all, and flout it.
X marks the spot to signal and shout it.
Take the news,
Reels, reviews,
And tell the troops to trumpet about it.

Everybody wants to be noted –
eXtraordinary, promoted.
Till they find
Reports rewind,
And soon they see their source was misquoted.

Face Value

Feign and fortune
Are fleeting.
Costumes
Entrap.

Vacant visages
Alert any:
Looks leave, but
Understanding
Endures.

Faith

Fleeting
Arguments are
Interrupted by
Truth and
Hope.

Favors

Friends and fellows may
Ask assistance:
Visiting our values
Or owning obligations to come?
Responses reveal our real regard,
Simple or sophisticated?

Fireworks

Flares and flashes,
Incandescence,
Rolling roars at
Evening's essence –
Wowing kids of every age,
Overhead, the rockets rage.
Reeking vapors now extend,
Keeping sleepless man's best friend.
Soon it stops. May sleep descend.

Futile

Flawed forms fail
Under purposeless existence.
Tell me why you breathe,
Imitating idealism for nothing. No!
Linger in love that lasts.
Eternity counts for everything.

Gaping

Glamour and glitz
Are accentuated,
Pitching paparazzi
Into interaction.
No one knows why
Gossip is glorified.

Gaslighter

Go ahead.
Adapt reality.
Stretch the story,
Like your elastic waistband.
Idolize yourself,
Going over and over your version.
History happened.
Truth tells in time.
Everyone's an eyewitness.
Roll tape at ten.

Good News

Glad greetings sit
Out of onlookers' eyes,
On a tidy shelf,
Daring me to peek again.

Needed on dark days,
Each treasured note in the box
Welcomes me back.
Soul restored.

Grace

Go forth.
Reach and rescue.
Any and all
Can call
Eternity.

Grey Matter Lost

Good and evil
Relays run.
Everybody
Yells for one.

Maybe many
Attitudes
Try to foster
Testy feuds,
Even banning
Reason's moods.

Losing battles
Overdone
Stretch to stress
Till none have won.

Hard as Nails

Holding out,
Autocratic always,
Rigid and relentless,
Dying to demand –

Anyone can
See his struggle.

Never knowing
Authority fails.
Inconsistent, insecure inside,
Losing love,
Still stubbornly standing.

Hogwash

Holy hogwash,
Only prattle,
Gibberish and giddiness –
Why do we bother?
Absurdity amuses,
So we scrawl scribbles of
Hooey and hot air – capturing clarity.

Holiness

Hoping to
Overachieve
Life's laws?
Imitating the Immortal?
No one need apply.
Exceptionality
Suffers when
Stabbed at by sons of men.

Hot Flash

Hark! Hark!
On fire here.
Temperature soars.

Fanning furiously,
Looking for air.
All clear again.
Shiny-sheeny.
Here come the chills.

How Great Thou Art

Heavenly Father,
Omnipotent One,
We worship You.

Glorious God,
Righteous Ruler,
Eternal Father,
All creation bows
To honor You.

Triumphant and true,
Holy and honored,
Only You are worthy,
Up above all.

Almighty and
Reigning
To You we sing.

Hope

However
Obstacles obfuscate,
Potential peeks perceptibly –
Everything entirely evolves eventually.

Humanity

How is it possible that
Understanding evades us?
Mankind is
Always seeming to
Need more
Information, but
Totally missing
Your point?

Inhaling the Sea

Into the surf we splash,
Never noticing
How strong the undertow may be.
All of a sudden,
Licentious lore
Is uplifted beneath our toes.
Now we are tossed,
Gulping briny breaths.

Time stops.
Hungry for air, we
Emerge at last.

Stronger than we knew.
Every wave now inspires
Awe and new respect.

It's Only Words

Indeed,
Terminology
Stings.

Obviously,
No one
Likes
Yacking and attacking.

We
Only
Ridicule and
Destroy with
Semantics.

Just My Imagination

Just
Under
Sight, is
Triumph.

Mark it
Yours.

In my own
Mind, I
Always
Gather
Insights and
Notions,
Appraising and approving
Totally of any
Initiative
Outpacing mere
Normalcy.

Juxtapose

Jumping
Under
eXtremes of
Truth,
Always
Pretending,
Opposites may
Seem
Equal.

Kissing

Kindness from above
Is ideal and
Sweetly sparkling, as
Sunshine simply
Inspires
New brightness and
Glow on my cheeks.

Launched Before Lunch

Loretta was lovely for sure,
Astride with her clean manicure,
Until underneath brewed a buck –
No warning, so quick, just her luck.
Catastrophe struck, as she flew,
Her helmet removed for her 'do.
Each onlooker stood, daring dread.
Does fashion count, heels over head?

At last, the equestrienne rose
Good grief! There she stood, wiping nose.
Another day she would return
In fashions pristine, cash to burn.
No true horse sense lessons to learn.

Library

Ledges and lofts
Imagine ideas,
Bound and determined.
Read me another;
Ask for a tale.
Return to reload:
Yarns without yawns.

Lilies

Life
Is
Lovely and
Inviting
Every
Springtime.

Linen Moments

Loads of laundry
Initiate insight.
Now I know
Each ounce of energy
Needs newness.

Making mindless mounds,
Overtaking unwashed sheets
May seem mundane,
Everlasting and unnoticed.
Nevertheless, each wrinkled wonder,
Transformed to freshness,
Signals a new start.

Love Me Tender

Let's linger awhile,
Only we two.
Velocities can wait;
Everything fades.

Maybe we can make a moment
Extend beyond experience.

Touch me with words,
Embracing our ears and hearts –
No need for nonsense.
Don't you hear it?
Each heart listens,
Ready for a rapt report.

Magnum Opus

Magnificent masterpiece.
Audiences applaud.
Greatness glistens,
Needing no introduction.
Understanding appears with
Mastery.

Only the most gifted
Perceive life purely,
Unless true artistry
Sets seekers to see it too.

Mattering

Making matter,
Adams from atoms –
Tending,
Trending
Ever after.
Rise, revive
Identity.
Nudge every nose to
Give a cry.

Maybe Mercy

Maybe we might mend this mess.
After all, we're bound to bless.
Yes, we're wrong,
But we belong.
Each madness may our bond impress.

Maligning may make mercy steep –
Each pain and grievance that we keep.
Rescue waits
Calls back the fates.
Yet fine forgiveness ne'er comes cheap.

Meditation

Meekness is might,
Empowered by purpose.
Daily deliverance
Is found in
Time spent in solace.
Attention is restored, and
Tranquility returned.
Inspiration is enlightened
Only in moments with
No interruptions.

Memories

Making memories
Every day
Makes us mindful
On the way.
Recognizing
In our dreams
Each day counts, or
So it seems.

Metaphysical

Maybe
Eternity
Takes time.
Apathy
Pretends
Hope is
Yielded.
Somehow
It seems
Contradictory.
After all, we
Live for love.

Mindful

Meditation
In a whirl –
Needful nation
Did unfurl.
Far past longing
Under test;
Let's just stop and take a rest.

Moonlight Melodies

Marvelous musings
Overtake us
On such glorious
Nights.
Lovely lighting
Interprets the world in
Glinting glory.
How we stare at the starry span.
Tonight is filled with promise.

Moonlight melodies mark the sky,
Embracing every ear in
Long-lost lore.
Only optimistic stories
Dare be told.
Into each heart
Evening spills its
Sweet song.

Morning Glory

Maybe
Only
Reveille
Needs
Initiate
New
Greetings –

Gladly
Lingering,
Overlooking
Remaining
Yearnings.

My Bad, Huh?

Maybe it's me;
Yeah, it's you.

Better yet,
Apologize in
Derision.

How about
Underdone
Humility?

Nemesis Named

No nature knows when it may need
Each prayer of purpose to proceed.
Mankind, mere mortals, may intend
Endearing legends to befriend.
Still strikes the savage, sending all
Into a frightful fated fall.
Strength fails in face of cancer's call.

Now nevermore may we declare
Adventure's boldness thus to bear.
Mistaken though we all may be,
Enduring memories our emcee,
Deliver hope's own guarantee.

News Media

Newsworthy and novel, so
Everyone might learn something
Worthy and weighty –
Sourced in substance.

Mannequins of mindsets,
Ever editorializing –
Don't you dare defy domains,
Initiating insight or
Advancing truth.

Niagara Falls

Nature is numbing.
Into the foam of
Astounding aqua,
Great gusts tumble.
Amazed onlookers
Roar in appreciation.
Ah, what wonder.

Falling is easy,
Although an eddy may
Leave us whirling.
Look up and
See the source of each splash.

Noodles

Noodles may seem
Only wiggly and
Obviously fragile.
Delightful and delectable.
Look, however.
Every man who uses his own is
Smarter than he who does not.

Not My Cup of Tea

No more for me, thanks.
Only one cup.
Testing new tastes is tricky.

Maybe next time
You can try my tastes.

Cups may overflow,
Unless we endure
Periodic possibilities.

Outside our own choices,
Favorites may flourish.

Till we sample
Every epicurean ideal,
Anyone may avoid a treasure.

Obtuse

Overlooking the obvious,

Baiting the curious,

Tremulous theories are tested.

Unless one is included,

Stories may be spelled, but

Everyone else escapes esoteric understanding.

One Foot in the Grave

Outstanding orders
Never negate
Eternity's call.

Final footsteps
Only lead
Outwards
To the unseen.

Individuals
Never know.

Temporality triumphs.
Holiness hollers for
Eternity's entrance.

Go for glory.
Resurrection is reserved,
As Almighty addresses with
Vicarious virtue,
Enlisting those who attend.

Oozing

Only for a moment,
Outwardly appealing,
Zealously alluring.
Inside, however,
Neurons fire falsely.
God only knows.

Optics

Outward appearances
Pilot the program,
Totally trend-focused,
In spite of ideals.
C'mon, folks.
Suppose we sample authenticity.

Observation

Outlooks
Build.
Senses
Evolve.
Rationalizations
Vanish.
Assumptions
Tumble.
Insight's an
Option –
Now that eyes are open.

Paris

Pondering La Tour Eiffel,
Always dreaming; time'll tell.
Reminisce.
In time we'll miss
Savored secrets hidden well.

Pawn

Placed in position,
Always at attention.
Warriors will wonder not –
Named by those they trust.

Persuasion

Please! Please! Please!
Enthusiasm entreats.
Resolution revels.
Stop and submit.
Underlings are all others.
All he asks is
Simple accord,
Insisting
Only his way.
No others matter.

Popcorn

Put on the popper;
Open the lid.
Pass it around, and
Crank up the vid.
Only ourselves
R-S-V-P.
Noshing, crunching, heartily.

Praise the Lord

Praise the Father,
Royal One,
And the Spirit,
Inner-One,
Sacred God,
Eternal Son.

Time before –
Hear Him roar
Ever more.

Laud Him always
Over all.
Raise His praises.
Death may fall.

Pray, Tell, Hush

Perhaps I need
Raw prayers to feed
An urgent plea –
You'll pray for me?

Then tell another, as a care;
Enjoy the passing, here and there.
Let everyone launch loose my tale.
Look! How the secret does prevail.

How weary must the Maker be,
Unvisited by you and me.
See, here He waits to hear our call,
How can we stick with gossip's gall?

Predictable

Ponderous

Routine -

Enduring

Drudgery -

Inexhaustible

Chores

Take away

Ambition,

Bringing

Little

Enthusiasm.

Privilege

Probably provocative, but
Reality resounds remarkably.
Identifying indemnifies
Virtually, vitally.
Ignoring isn't innocent.
Let's look and learn.
Everyone matters, but equally?
Good God, get us going.
Everyone needs to make it so.

Query First

Quick! Editor!
Under your stack,
Each line and phrase
Risks your attack.
You'll call me back?

Find in your heart –
I'm sure you can.
Reply delighted.
Send a plan
To understand.

Quilts

Quietly crawling
Underneath
Innumerable
Layers of
Treasured threads –
Solace.

Reincarnation

Returning to origins,
Everything takes turns.
Into the Creator's hands,
No one may deny.
Can we see the future
And what form it will take?
Rebirth and renewal
Name our deepest hope.
Almighty! We cry out to You.
Take our tired limbs
Into Your tireless ones.
Only You hold power of life and death.
Never let us go.

Schism

Skipping sense,
Conflicts are created.
How does it happen?
Individualities emerge.
Semantics and specifics supplant
Mercy's good measure.

Seasons

So they come, and so they go,
Every cycle, every show.
As we live each stage, may we
Stop and sense the world with glee.
Only faster, do they pass.
None has pow'r to make them last.
So worry not on that forecast!

Sensuality

Setting spirit and soul aside,
Entertainment intervenes.
Now trumps not yet.
Sensations replace sense,
Utter pleasure the goal.
Anyone can see
Liberty equals not license.
In an instant,
Total fantasy
Yields far less than we expected.

Shoelaces

Slightest stumbles
Hinder me.
Oh, my God,
Enlighten, free.
Looking down,
At last, I see
Clipping, clopping,
Empties glee.
Stop, retie, and let it be.

Sneakers

Simple steps
Need not noodle
Expert explanations
Anyway.
Kicking off calories
Every time
Rallies returns, or
So she said.

Solitude

Sometimes
Only
Loneliness
Imparts
Truth,
Understanding,
Determination and
Endurance.

Spent

Stop me, if you've heard this.
Pouring out my pep.
Evermore,
Nevermore,
Treading towards misstep.

Spice

Savory scents
Pique the palate,
Inviting inspiration –
Cuisine capers.
Epicureans enjoy.

Spring

Shivering, as the last snow falls,
Pulling on my overalls,
Reaching for each garden glove,
I'm itching for the sun's warm love.
Never doubting, I can say,
"Gentle days are on the way."

Spring Showers Renew

Stubborn
Pique
Remains
Intact,
Negating
Gentleness.

Someday,
Humbly,
Obeisant,
We
Encounter
Reinvigorating
Strength.

Rising,
Energized,
New –
Each
Wonders.

Stalker

Suspicious shadows stop,
Total obscured by trees.
Almost not breathing, she tiptoes,
Losing her footing and stumbling, but
Keeping to the paved path.
Every twig echoes of peril,
Racing her home.

Stargazing

Slip from sight
To catch a glance –
All is right
Regarding chance.
Gesture higher;
Angels smile.
Zeal inspired
In a while.
Night brings even
Glints of Heaven.

Summer

Savoring these warmer days,
Underneath the sun's warm gaze,
My skin has gained a healthy glow.
My outlook says, "Get up, and go!"
Everybody has a blast,
Regretting balmy days won't last.

Supernatural

Surely, an

Unseen

Person

Eternal

Reigns.

Natural

Appearances

Truth is

Undermined, but

Right relationship

Always

Lasts.

Surprise! Surprise!

Some squirrels may be wiser than gents,
Untempted to toss their two cents –
Refusing to bend others' ears
Pretending, denying their fears.
Ridiculous as it may sound,
I wonder, when no one's around:
Since squirrels scurry fast out of sight,
Each girl may find squirrels more polite.

So what is surprising in that,
Unless we consider a chat?
Respect most resistant may flee,
Perhaps like a squirrel up a tree.
Reminders send tails in the air;
I wonder if folks even care.
So sudden may scurriers race,
Eluding maturity's face.

Survivor

Staying power,
Undergirded by
Resolve.
Vigor lasts.
Integrity endures.
Viable values
Outrun mere
Reputation.

Sweat Equity

Somehow sweat
Works wonders wild –
Every session's
Assets piled
Till vices are viled.

Enjoyment, effort
Quickly wield
Unseen upticks
In the field
Till we reap a
Youthful yield.

Sweets and Eats

Stay far away from sugared treat,
Warns dentist, doctor, all I meet.
Each day, resolved to curb the urge,
Eyes aimed to stop the snacking splurge –
Till nighttime cravings stop me short,
Send my convictions to abort.

Aghast, as from the binge I crash,
No vict'ry here, my teeth I gnash.
Day one begins with dawn's first flash.

Each day, I run a pile of miles,
As calories bring fitness trials.
Tomorrow, I'll be better armed,
Though by indulgence I be charmed.

Swerving

So swish and swerve,
Whoa, no! a curve!
Each hand turns ash;
Regrip, don't crash.
Veer left and right,
In frenzied fright.
Now off we go:
Go full speed. Go!

Teatimes

Trust us.
Everyone's all ears,
Attentive and alert at
The tea table.
It's your turn.
"My lips are sealed,"
Everyone promises.
Still, are we sure?

Thanksgiving

Truly, I am thankful, blessed –
Heaven knows no second best.
All my life, Provider knows.
Needs unspoken, mercy flows.
King of life, grant gratitude,
Save me from my attitude.
Give me graciousness and peace
In Your image – mine release.
Victory, my highest goal,
Inconsistent is my soul.
Now I need You most of all,
Grant me strength to heed Your call.

The Color Purple

Tints and
Hues may
Exchange.

Cast an
Outward
Look
Over the
Rainbow.

Purple is
Understood as
Royalty,
Properly
Left to
Elegance.

Third Party

Taking
Hold,
Interfering,
Rejecting
Discernment.

Perhaps
Anyone
Refuses
Truth's
Yardstick.

To Be or Not to Be

Try to tell
Outright untruths.

Before long,
Everything is revealed.

Only in living may
Recognition return.

No one may know
Our own souls by
Trying to tease the truth.

Try to tell
Outright untruths.

Before long,
Everything is fulfilled.

Touch Base Again

Tap the keyboard,
Out of time.
Understanding
Calls are prime.
How long's it been?

Bounce a message,
As you go.
Stop to step on
Ego's toe.

All we ask is
Give a sec
Anytime you
Itch to check –
Not where or when.

Tropical Depression

Thunder calls,
Raining blues
Onto all weaker
Promises below.
Inside their souls,
Characters
Await the
Light of hope.

Dousing cheer,
Every drop dips,
Pouring weight
Right to the core of
Every hardened heart.
Stop the downfall!
Save the sodden ones
In time for
Overtures of bright
New days.

Turtles

Trotting
Under the
Radar
Till
Longer legs
Enjoy
Success.

Unforgettable

Umbrellas unseen
Never cast shadows,
Folding freely and
Opening over
Reminiscences and reveries.
Glorious gifts,
Every one.
Times treasured and
Troves of truth
Always are illuminated
Because their brightness
Leaves vestiges of value
Everywhere.

Unfriended Again

Unwound, untied –
No place to hide.
Friendship is lost;
Remove the cost.
It seems a rift
Expands the drift.
No time for talk,
Decide to walk.
Enough's enough,
Dumped in a huff.

Another time?
Go, gossip's grime.
And any ear
Inclined to hear,
Never come near.

Vacation

Verge of panic –
Assembling the family,
Car fully loaded.
Arriving at last,
Toting luggage
Into new surroundings.
Only one week –
Need much longer.

Vaccine Saga

Virtually vexed,
Anyone might wonder if
Common complaints
Could be contained by
Ideals immunization.
Nobody needs to know.
Everyone would be enhanced.

Scratch that.
Allowing across-the-board action
Goes against the grain of
All but those in absolute authority.

Walking on Eggshells

Weak-kneed worry,
Always anticipating
Leers and sneers.
Knowing not
If this time
No one can
Guarantee safety.

On the outside,
Nothing seems wrong.

Eggshells crack,
Giving way to
Ghastly
Scenes.
Havens turn to
Enmity.
Love is
Lost,
Sadly surrendered.

War and Peace

Winning and losing
Are all about
Rebellion and rights.

Awareness
Needs a
Dream.

Postwar
Establishment
Absolutely
Costs
Everything.

Weeping Willows

Weighing in,
Every ramification
Expresses emotion –
Perhaps postulating on
Inspiration, but
Never
Giving all to gravity.

Weeping willows
Initiate introspection.
Look how we long for
Lighter loads,
Only we never see
Why weighty works
Seem to grow us.

What a Wonderful World

Why whine?
Holy heartache.
All around us,
Truth tolls.

Alleluia.

What wonders –
Only observe.
Needless nagging
Drags us down.
Eternity echoes
Resounding rolls of
Fabulosity and favor,
Under an umbrella of
Love that lasts.

Watch and wait.
Overcomers' outlook
Revives the rest.
Look, He comes,
Dancing on the dawn.

Whatever

Writing off worries,
Hurried and hassled,
Avoids oversharing.
Total turnoff –
Every extended effort
Verily voided,
Emptied of expression,
Repelling reason.

Wilderness

Where are we?

I imagined such a place,

Long ago.

Did we depart for a distance?

Everything seems eerie, though

Relics remain.

Never did we need

Escape from the everyday.

Somehow, sanity stays

Safely ensconced, since we skipped her step.

Winter

When the earth is hard and cold,
Icy sidewalks are patrolled.
Never daunted, children romp,
Tucking pants in boots, they clomp.
Each and every frozen pace
Reveals a chilly, rosy face.

Writing

Winsome words
Rarely recall requirements.
Instead, inspiration
Tangles with truth,
Inciting introspection.
Never negate
Great glimpses engaged.

Youth

Yesterday, so young in haste –
Only back then, adulthood chased.
Until, it came. Waist fell to waste.
Things tumbled out, from place to place
Help! How my youth has been erased.

Zest

Zealous living
Employs energy.
Standing still
Takes too much time.

GOING VERTICAL: ACROSTICS IN ACTION

About the Author

An award-winning poet and prolific writer, holding a B.A. in English and an M.S. in Journalism, Linda Ann Nickerson has worked as a professional writer for more than four decades.

She has also taught creative writing, poetry, and literature classes and has presented to adult writing workshops and groups.

In an earlier life, she worked as a book editor and widely-read reviewer of books on all types of topics.

Linda Ann writes news and feature columns for several well-known websites. Her published portfolio includes well over 5,000 web articles, as well as countless print pieces.

When she's not writing poetry, fiction, news, features, or promotional copy, Linda Ann may be found riding horses, running canine cross-country, biking country trails, stitching up a quilt, or training for her next marathon. Or she may simply have her nose buried in another book.

Other poetry books by Linda Ann Nickerson include:

- *ABCs of Acrostic Poetry: The keyword is king*

- *Absent Nightmare Zinnias: Rhymed Acrostics from A to Z*

- *Fashion Victims: Missing Style by a Marvelous Mile*

- *Horseplay Secrets: Learning in Rhyme from Equines Sublime*

- *Stealing Wonder: A Rhyming Race to Capture Grace*

- *What's in Santa's Sleigh This Christmas?*

GOING VERTICAL: ACROSTICS IN ACTION

www.ingramcontent.com/pod-product-compliance
Lightning Source LLC
LaVergne TN
LVHW091259080426
835510LV00007B/320